Manners at the Table

by **Carrie Finn**   illustrated by **Chris Lensch**

PiCTURE WiNDOW BOOKS
Minneapolis, Minnesota

Special thanks to our advisers for their expertise:

Kay Augustine, Associate Director
Institute for Character Development at Drake University

Susan Kesselring, M.A., Literacy Educator
Rosemount–Apple Valley–Eagan (Minnesota) School District

Editor: Nick Healy
Designer: Tracy Davies
Page Production: Melissa Kes
Art Director: Nathan Gassman
Associate Managing Editor: Christianne Jones
The illustrations in this book were created digitally.

Picture Window Books
1710 Roe Crest Drive
North Mankato, Minnesota 56003
www.capstonepub.com

Library of Congress Cataloging-in-Publication Data
Finn, Carrie.
Manners at the table / by Carrie Finn ; illustrated by Chris Lensch.
p. cm. — (Way to be!)
Includes bibliographical references and index.
ISBN-13: 978-1-4048-3155-1 (library binding)
ISBN-13: 978-1-4048-3553-5 (paperback)
1. Table etiquette—Juvenile literature. 2. Etiquette for children and
teenagers—Juvenile literature. I. Lensch, Chris. II. Title.
BJ2041.F56 2007
395.5'4—dc22   2006027567

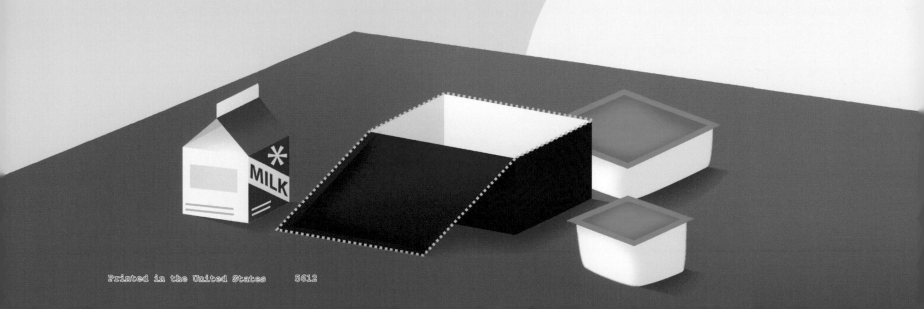

Good manners make mealtime a happy time for everyone. In a restaurant, you can use good manners to show respect for the cook, your server, and other customers. At home, your manners show respect for your family members.

There are lots of ways to use good manners at the table.

Lucy washes her hands with soap before she comes to the table.

She is using good manners.

Peter puts his napkin in his lap. He sits still and stays in his chair during the meal.

He is using good manners.

Georgia takes small bites of her food.

She is using good manners.

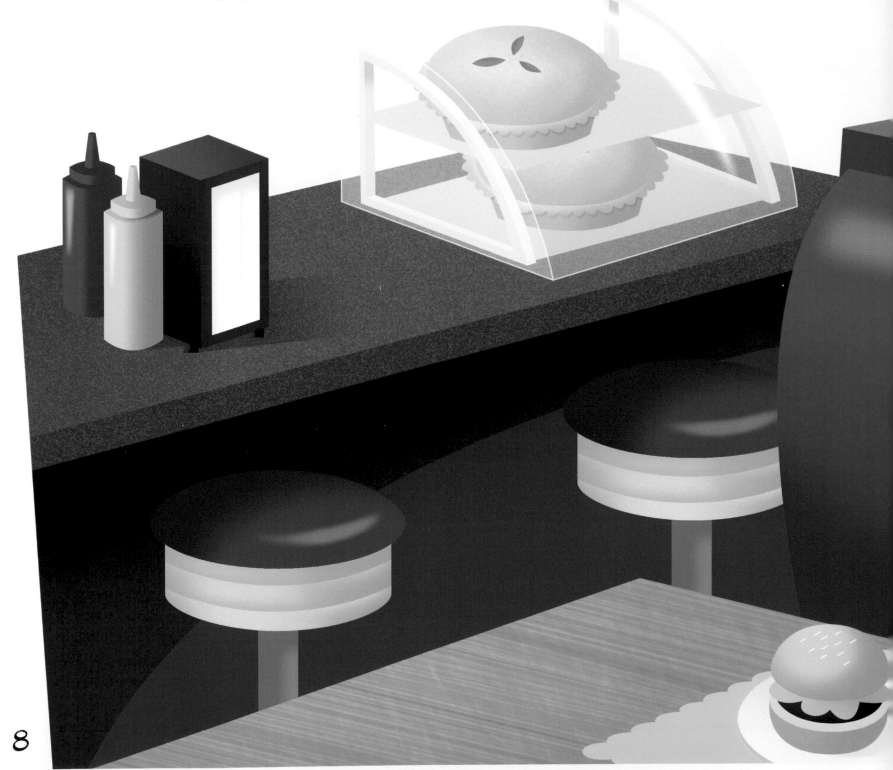

Ron keeps his mouth closed
while he chews his food.

**He is using
good manners.**

April sips her milk slowly instead of gulping it down.

She is using good manners.

Billy says "Please" when he asks Becca to pass the butter. He says "Thank you" when she does.

He is using
good manners.

Daniel is not sure he will like today's lunch. Still, he tastes everything on his plate.

He is using good manners.

Teddy uses his napkin to wipe his mouth. He never wipes his mouth on his shirt.

He is using good manners.

Sarah and Isaac ask to be excused from the table at the end of the meal.

They are using good manners.

Try using your good manners whenever you sit down to eat. Good manners allow everyone to relax and enjoy the meal.

Fun Facts

In Senegal, it is not polite to make eye contact with others while eating.

In Vietnam, making loud noises, such as slurping your soup from the bowl, shows you like your meal.

In the United States, it is rude to burp at the table, but in some countries, burping shows appreciation for the food.

In some African countries, men and women eat their meals separately.

In some parts of Cameroon, people use their right hands to eat out of a big bowl shared by everyone.

In Norway, many people eat four meals a day. Some people eat five a day.

To Learn More

At the Library

DeGezelle, Terri. *Manners at a Restaurant*. Mankato, Minn.: Capstone Press, 2004.

Helmer, Diana Star. *The Cat Who Came for Tacos*. Morton Grove, Ill.: Albert Whitman, 2003.

Raschka, Chris, and Vladimir Radunsky. *Table Manners*. Cambridge, Mass.: Candlewick, 2001.

On the Web

FactHound offers a safe, fun way to find Web sites related to this book.
All of the sites on FactHound have been researched by our staff.

1. Visit *www.facthound.com*

2. Type in this special code: 140483155X

3. Click on the FETCH IT button.

Your trusty FactHound will fetch the best sites for you!

Index

Look for all of the books in the Way to Be! series:

Being a Good Citizen: A Book About Citizenship

Being Fair: A Book About Fairness

Being Respectful: A Book About Respectfulness

Being Responsible: A Book About Responsibility

Being Trustworthy: A Book About Trustworthiness

Caring: A Book About Caring

Manners at School

Manners at the Table

Manners in Public

Manners in the Library

Manners on the Playground

Manners on the Telephone